WELCOME TO GOLF BIOGRAPHIES FOR KIDS

Paragon Publishing offers a wide selection of other sports biographies and quiz books, so be sure to check them out if you enjoy this one.

Paragon Publishing is a privately run publishing company which cares greatly about the accuracy of its content.

As many facts and figures in this book are subject to change, please email us at **ParagonPublishing23@gmail.com** if you notice any inaccuracies to help us keep our book as up-to-date and as accurate as possible.

If you have enjoyed this book please leave us a review on Amazon.

Have fun!

CONTENTS

INTRODUCTION

This book will take a look at the 25 greatest golfers to ever play the great game. You will learn how each of these legends started playing golf as a child, and then all the great things they achieved over their careers. Some of these golfers played a very long time ago, so there may even be names that you do not recognise or do not know much about.

Before we delve into some of the greatest golfers to ever play the game, let's take a brief look at its history and how golf got to be where it is today. Golf originated on the east coast of Scotland in an area close to the royal capital of Edinburgh in the 15th century, although the game looked very different compared to today. In the early days, players would attempt to hit a pebble over sand dunes and around tracks using a bent club or stick. People loved the sport so much that it was banned by King James II because it was distracting people from their military training.

This ban was lifted in 1502 and King James soon brought the game to England and Mary Queen of Scots, who then brought the game to France (the term caddie refers to the name for her French military aides; cadets). The first international golf match was held in Edinburgh in 1682 with the Scots coming out on top playing against the English.

Golf officially became a sport when the Gentlemen Golfers of Leith created the first club in 1744. Soon after this, the first 18 hole course was constructed at St Andrews in 1764.

At this time, golfers used hand-made wooden clubs and balls were made from compressed feathers wrapped in a stitched horse hide.

During the 19th century golf started to spread across the world as the British Empire continued to expand. The first golf club outside of Britain was created in 1820 in Bangalore, India. Others around the world quickly followed, and by the end of the 19th century there were golf clubs in Ireland, Australia, South Africa and many more countries.

The United States Golf Association (USGA) formed in 1894, and by 1900 more than 1000 golf clubs had appeared in the USA. The PGA Tour soon followed in 1929 and the rest is history.

Golf quickly grew from a small sport played in Scotland, where pebbles where hit over sand dunes, to become one of the biggest sports the world has ever seen. Today it is estimated that 66 million people play golf worldwide!

From all the millions of people who have ever played the game, this book has selected the 25 greatest players of all time. Being called one of the GOAT's (Greatest Of All Time) is a very big claim to make and there are many factors that must be ticked for a player to even be considered in this bracket. It is not just about the player with the best swing, or the players with the most majors won, but it is also about their ability to consistently perform week in week out for years or even decades, and to leave a legacy upon the sport.

TIGER WOODS

MAJORS WON

The Masters	🏆	X5
PGA Championship	🏆	X4
US Open	🏆	X3
The Open	🏆	X3

PGA TOUR VICTORIES	PRO VICTORIES
82	109

Full Name	Eldrick Tont Woods
Nickname	Tiger
Nationality	American
Turned Pro	1996

CHILDHOOD

Eldrick Tont "Tiger" Woods was born in Cypress, California to Earl, a retired US Army Officer and Vietnam Veteran, and Kultida "Tida" Woods. A child prodigy, he was introduced to golf before the age of two by his father, a single digit handicap player in his own right and a college baseball player.

Whilst still a young boy, he appeared alongside the comedian Bob Hope on a TV show as a star of the future, and regularly featured in golf magazines. He first broke 80 at the age of eight, and was soon winning national championships and competing with players much older than him, some of whom were professionals. At 15 he became the youngest ever US Junior Amateur Champion and defended his title the following year, also making his PGA tour debut.

Woods enrolled at Stanford University under a golf scholarship, whilst winning three consecutive US Amateur Championships. He competed in his first major, the 1996 Masters, and won the silver medal at the British Open as the leading amateur. He turned professional at the age of 20.

GOLF CAREER

Woods took the world of golf by storm, and by 1997, he had won three PGA Tour events as well as his first major - the Masters. Later that same year, he became the world number one ranked player, and between 1999 and 2004, occupied top spot for 264 weeks consecutively. He would then beat this streak by being ranked number 1 from June 2005 to October 2010 for 281 consecutive weeks. By this point, he had won 14 majors and most observers believed it was a matter of when, and not if he would surpass Jack Nicklaus' record of major wins.

However, off the course issues began to intrude, and he took a self-imposed break from golf for five months to deal with his marital breakdown. His world ranking slumped before he once again regained top spot, but then he began to experience severe problems with his back, and between 2014 and 2017, he underwent four separate surgeries. He did recover enough to win his first major in 11 years at the 2019 Masters, but that looks like it will be his last.

In February 2021, Woods was involved in a serious car accident that almost killed him. He underwent emergency surgery to repair compound fractures and spent many weeks in hospital. He has since indicated that his career as a professional golfer is likely over, although he will continue to play the occasional event.

GREATEST ACHIEVEMENTS IN GOLF

- Woods is second on the all-time list of major winners (behind Jack Nicklaus).
- Many golf commentators believe he is the best "closer" in history, having a 14-1 record going into the final round of a major with a share of the lead at least.
- He has won 82 PGA tour events, which is a record he holds with Sam Snead, and eleven more that Nicklaus.
- He also has 41 European Tour wins, and 24 in other tournaments, in addition to the 21 amateur victories he achieved.

- He has the lowest career scoring average and has won more money than anybody in the history of the PGA Tour.
- Woods has been PGA Player of the Year 11 times, has been the leading money winner ten times, the Vardon Trophy winner nine times, and the Byron Nelson Award winner nine times – all records.
- He has hit 20 holes in one, his first coming at the age of just six.
- His 498-yard drive at the par 5 18th at the Plantation Course in Kapalua Resort, Hawaii, in 2002 is the longest recorded drive in the history of the PGA Tour.

GREATEST QUOTES

"Winning is not always the barometer of success."

"You can win all the tournaments you want but the majors are what you're remembered for. It's how you're measured as a champion in our sport. The majors are where it's at."

"People don't understand that when I grew up, I was never the most talented. I was never the biggest. I was never the fastest. I certainly was never the strongest. The only thing I had was my work ethic, and that's what has gotten me this far".

TOM WATSON

MAJORS WON

The Masters	🏆	X2
PGA Championship	🏆	X0
US Open	🏆	X1
The Open	🏆	X5

PGA TOUR VICTORIES	PRO VICTORIES
39	70

Full Name	Thomas Sturges Watson
Nickname	Huckleberry Dillinger
Nationality	American
Turned Pro	1971

CHILDHOOD

Watson was born in Kansas City, Missouri, and was introduced to the game of golf by his father, Ray. He first gained local prestige playing for his high school team and then won four Missouri State Amateur Championships. He attended Stanford University, where he played on their golf and table tennis teams, and graduated with a degree in psychology. He joined the PGA tour in 1971.

GOLF CAREER

It took Watson three years to win his first PGA tour title at the Western Open, and clinched his first major victory - the British Open - the following year. He quickly became the dominant player in world golf of his time. 1980 was arguably the peak of his career when he won the British Open, six events in America and had 16 top ten finishes on the PGA Tour.

His successes began to tail off in the late 1980s when he began to develop putting problems, although after a nine-year gap without a win, he won the Memorial Tournament in 1996 and the MasterCard Colonial the following year. He then switched to the Champions Tour, where he won 14 tournaments, including six majors. At the age of 68, despite no longer competing in the main event, he won the Masters Tournament Par-3 contest; the oldest man ever to do so.

The author of a number of books on the sport, Watson has been an outspoken critic of the amount of prize money in golf, believing that it corrupts the desire of some players rather than them trying to be the best they can.

GREATEST ACHIEVEMENTS IN GOLF:

- Watson was the number one ranked player in the world from 1978 to 1982, and the number two behind Seve Ballesteros in the two following years.
- Five times he was the leading money winner on the PGA Tour, and was named PGA Player of the Year on six occasions.
- He won eight major championships (five British Opens, two Masters and the US Open), and finished his career with 70 professional wins. Watson is regarded as one of the best links' players of all-time.
- He had a long-standing rivalry with Jack Nicklaus that helped boost the popularity of the sport.
- Between 1977 and 1979 he won the Vardon Trophy for the lowest scoring average on the PGA Tour.
- He is the only player to have scored a round of 67 or fewer in all four majors at least once in five different decades.
- He played on four Ryder Cup teams and spectacularly took them to success in 1983 at The Belfry by contributing 4 points.
- Watson was inducted into the World Golf Hall of Fame in 1988, a year after receiving the Bob Jones Award for distinguished sportsmanship in golf.
- He is the oldest player to win after any completed round of a major championship.

GREATEST QUOTES

"Golf is a game of ego, but it is also a game of integrity: the most important thing is you do what's right when no one is looking".

RORY MCILROY

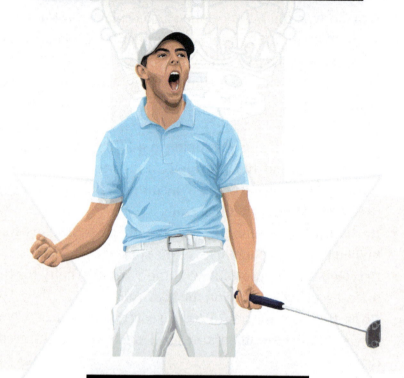

MAJORS WON

The Masters	🏆	X0
PGA Championship	🏆	X2
US Open	🏆	X1
The Open	🏆	X1

PGA TOUR VICTORIES	PRO VICTORIES
20	32

Full Name	Rory McIlroy
Nickname	Rory, Wee-Mac
Nationality	Northern Irish
Turned Pro	2007

CHILDHOOD

McIlroy was born in Hollywood, Northern Ireland. He is the only child of Gerry McIlroy and Rosie McDonald. It was his father who introduced him to golf when he was still very young, and coached him. He was given a golf club as a present and loved it so much that he used to take it to bed with him. He joined Hollywood Golf Club aged just seven, and began working with the club professional, Michael Bannon, who would go on to become his coach and mentor.

By the time he was 15, McIlroy was playing for Ireland and Europe in international competitions, and in 2006 he became the European Amateur Champion. The following year he won the Silver Medal as the leading amateur at the Open Championship in Carnoustie. He turned professional in 2007.

GOLF CAREER

After finishing third and tied for fourth place in two tournaments that year, McIlroy became the youngest ever player to earn a European Tour card. His first professional win came in 2009 when he won the Dubai Desert Open aged just 19. In 2011, he led the Masters after the third round, but a final back nine cost him his chance. However, a few months later he announced himself to the golf world by winning the US Open by 8 strokes, setting a new 72-hole record for the tournament in the process, and becoming the youngest winner since Bobby Jones.

The following year he won the PGA Championship, and in 2014

he made it 4 victories in majors by winning the British Open and the PGA Championship once again. He joined Jack Nicklaus and Tiger Woods in becoming the only men to win four majors by the age of 25.

Since his second PGA Championship, there have been no more majors, although time is still on his side. His most recent wins came in 2021 clinching both the Wells Fargo Championship and the CJ Cup by one stroke. He missed out on the 2022 Dubai Desert Classic by one stroke, after hitting his second shot on the final hole into the water.

GREATEST ACHIEVEMENTS IN GOLF

- McIlroy has won 20 tournaments so far on the PGA tour, 14 in Europe, and six other events. He was ranked the world number one amateur at the age of just 17, and would later become the number one ranked professional golfer in the world, holding top spot for 106 weeks.
- In 2011, he became the youngest golfer to win €10 million on the European Tour, and has twice been leading money winner on the PGA tour.
- In 2012 he scooped a number of awards: he was named PGA Player of the Year; won the Vardon Trophy for the lowest scoring average on the PGA tour (an award he has won three times); won the Byron Nelson award and the prestigious Laureus World Sports Award.
- He has three times been named European Tour Golfer of the Year, and won the Race to Dubai Championship on three occasions.
- He has made six appearances in the Ryder Cup for Europe to date, finishing on the winning team four times.

GREATEST QUOTES

"As long as I keep enjoying my golf, then hopefully I'll be able to play well".

PETER THOMSON

MAJORS WON

The Masters	🏆	X0
PGA Championship	🏆	X0
US Open	🏆	X0
The Open	🏆	X5

PGA TOUR VICTORIES	CAREER VICTORIES
6	98

Full Name	Peter William Thomson
Nickname	The Melbourne Tiger
Nationality	Australian
Turned Pro	1949

CHILDHOOD

Thomson was born in Melbourne, Australia. His father worked as a greenskeeper and he encouraged his son to take up the game. His first golf was played on a local public course. At the age of 12 he was given a two iron as a gift, and within four years, he had become area champion.

He studied at Victoria University, graduating with a degree in chemistry, although his passion was really geology. His knowledge of this would become useful in later years when the company he founded began to build golf courses in different parts of the world. Thomson turned professional in 1949, after giving up his role as an industrial chemist.

GOLF CAREER

He quickly achieved success on the professional tour, winning the first of his nine New Zealand Opens in 1950. He made his first appearance at the British Open in 1951, and the following year finished second, beginning a seven-year run where he either won the tournament or finished runner-up.

In 1953 and 1954, he switched to the PGA tour but did not have the same success. After this he mainly restricted himself to playing in Europe, Asia, Australia and New Zealand. His win at the British Open in 1965 was regarded as his most important, because unlike his early triumphs, all the world's best were there. Between 1966 and 1984, Thomson made 15 more appearances at the Open before switching to the PGA Seniors tour, winning nine times in 1985 and finishing top of the money list.

His last tournament victory was in 1988. Thomson was an active golf writer for half a century and designed more than one hundred golf courses, not only in Australia but around the world.

GREATEST ACHIEVEMENTS IN GOLF

- Thomson has been described as the finest links player of the modern era, and he had a particular affinity with St. Andrews, where he won the Claret Jug in 1955. He later bought a home in the city and received an honorary doctorate from St. Andrews University.
- He was often called upon by the locals to raise a toast in the clubhouse.
- He won the British Open five times, including three years in a row between 1954 and 1956 - the only man in history to win a Major three times in a row.
- His tournament wins included 26 in Europe, 11 in Asia, and 19 in Australia and New Zealand.
- In 1988, he was inducted into the World Golf Hall of Fame and the Sport Australia equivalent in 1985.
- Thomson was President of the Australian PGA between 1962 and 1964, helping to set up the Asian Tour, and at the 1998 Presidents' Cup, he was a victorious non-playing captain.
- He was made an OBE in 1957 and a CBE 23 years later, and in 2002 was made an Officer of the Order of Australia for services to golf.

GREATEST QUOTES

"The difference between winning and losing is always a mental one".

"Use your brain, not your endurance."

NICK FALDO

MAJORS WON

The Masters	🏆	X3
PGA Championship	🏆	X0
US Open	🏆	X0
The Open	🏆	X3

PGA TOUR VICTORIES	PRO VICTORIES
9	41

Full Name	Sir Nicholas Alexander Faldo
Nickname	Sir Nick
Nationality	English
Turned Pro	1976

CHILDHOOD

Faldo was born in Welwyn Garden City in Hertfordshire. He was not brought up with the game, but became hooked after watching Jack Nicklaus playing in the 1971 Masters on his parents' colour TV. Within three years, he had qualified to play in the English Amateur Championship, and a year later played in the Commonwealth Tournament in South Africa.

His prowess was noticed in the United States and he was awarded a golf scholarship by the University of Houston, but left after less than three months because he feared that going to school was interfering with his game. He turned professional in 1976 and joined the European Professional Golfer's Association.

GOLF CAREER

In 1977, he claimed his first European Tour victory and also made the first of his record 11 appearances in the Ryder Cup, becoming the youngest ever at that time to compete in the event. Over the coming few years, he developed a reputation as a steady player; one who was always in contention for the big prizes, but never quite good enough to seal the deal.

Faldo took the decision to re-work his swing with coach David Leadbetter, and the hard work paid off as he won his first major in 1987 - the British Open - where he scored 18 pars in the final round. Two more Opens and three Masters followed, the most famous victory of all coming at Augusta in 1996. Going into the final round he trailed Greg Norman by six shots, but still managed to overhaul the Australian.

As he entered his forties, his form gradually declined and he spent more time on off-course activities, particularly golf course design. He also began a successful broadcast career, becoming the leading golf analyst for CBS Sports and working for the BBC as well. Never the most popular man among his peers, British golf writer Peter Dobereiner suggested that Faldo was "obsessively driven by the impossible dream of technical perfection".

GREATEST ACHIEVEMENTS IN GOLF

- Faldo won six majors - the most by any European player in the modern era. He was the top ranked player in the world for 91 weeks.
- He achieved 41 professional wins in his career, including 30 victories on the European tour.
- He was named PGA Tour Player of the Year in 1990, and the European Player of the Year three times.
- Faldo played in a record 11 Ryder Cups and is one of the most successful players ever in the history of the competition, having won 25 points. In 2008, he captained the team, although his side lost on that occasion.
- His career earnings totaled over US $8 million.
- A member of the World Golf Hall of Fame, he was knighted by Queen Elizabeth in 2009.

GREATEST QUOTES

"Golf is not about the quality of your good shots, it is about the quality of your bad shots".

"When you are playing great, it is wonderful. Because you and your partner just want to go out and go "Who we got?" and off you go. But when you are playing badly, or your trust is dented, or your self-belief is gone, it's the worst (freaking) week in the world."

MICKEY WRIGHT

MAJORS WON

Western Open	🏆	X3
Titleholders Championship	🏆	X2
Women's PGA Championship	🏆	X4
US Women's Open	🏆	X4

LPGA TOUR VICTORIES	PRO VICTORIES
82	90

Full Name	Mary Kathryn Wright
Nickname	Mickey
Nationality	American
Turned Pro	1954

CHILDHOOD

Mary Kathryn Wright was born in San Diego, California. She began playing golf at the age of 12, and in 1952 she won the US Golfing Association's Junior Championship. She attended Stanford University and played for their golf team, but left after one year to devote herself to the game. In 1954, she won the World Amateur Championship, and was the lowest scoring amateur at the US Open before turning professional later that same year.

GOLF CAREER

Between 1958 and 1968 she recorded 79 out of her 82 LPGA victories, and was the dominant female player of the 1960s. In 1961, she won three of the four majors and two years later, won more than 40% of the tournaments she entered. She holds the record for the most wins in a single season. In 1966, Wright became the only player in LPGA history to win the LPGA Championship four times. In 1966, she won 11 events and was one of the original inductees into the LPGA Hall of Fame when it was created the following year.

However in 1969, at the age of 34, she stopped playing regularly for a variety of reasons which included foot problems, a fear of flying, and an aversion to sunlight. She played occasionally after that, and continued to play golf recreationally into old age. A breast cancer survivor, she died of a heart attack aged 85.

GREATEST ACHIEVEMENTS IN GOLF

- Second only to Kathy Whitworth in terms of LPGA titles won (82 compared to 98), Wright is the only player in the history of the game to hold all four LPGA major titles at the same time, having won the US Women's Open and the LPGA Championship in 1961, and then the Titleholders Championship and the Western Open the following year.
- Her 14-year winning streak has been bettered only by Whitworth.
- She topped the LPGA money list for four consecutive seasons between 1961 and 1964, and finished in the top ten thirteen times in her professional career.
- She was a five-time recipient of the Vare Trophy for the best scoring average on tour.
- Ben Hogan described Wright's swing as the best he had ever seen. This helped her to be a powerful hitter capable of 300-yard drives.
- One of her greatest rounds came at the Tall City Open in 1964 when she shot a final round of 62. Not only was it the lowest score in LPGA history at the time, but it was also four better than the men's record on the same course. She also made history by coming from 10 shots down to win, another record.
- She was inducted into the World Golf Hall of Fame in 1976 and the PGA of America Hall of Fame in 2017.

GREATEST QUOTES

"When I play my best golf, I feel as if I'm in a fog, standing back watching the earth in orbit with a golf club in my hands".

"But there is a difference between playing well and hitting the ball well. Hitting the ball well is about thirty per cent of it. The rest is being comfortable with the different situations on the course."

LEE TREVINO

MAJORS WON

The Masters	🏆	X0
PGA Championship	🏆	X2
US Open	🏆	X2
The Open	🏆	X2

PGA TOUR VICTORIES	PRO VICTORIES
29	92

Full Name	Lee Buck Trevino
Nickname	Supermex
Nationality	American
Turned Pro	1960

CHILDHOOD

Born into a family of Mexican ancestry, Trevino was raised by his mother, Juanita and his grandfather. He never knew his father. At the age of five, he started working in the cotton fields, and was introduced to golf by an uncle who gave him a few old clubs and some balls. He left school at the age of 14 and earned money as a caddie and also as a shoe shine boy.

When he was 17, he enrolled in the United States Marine Corps and spent four years in the army, spending part of his time playing golf with other officers and also competing in Armed Forces golf events.

GOLF CAREER

After his discharge from the Army, he began to work as a club professional in Texas, making extra money on the side by gambling. He qualified for the US Open in 1966, made the cut and by the following year, was successful enough to gain his entry onto the Tour. In the space of three weeks in 1971, he won the British, Canadian, and US Open titles, and the following year became the first player since Arnold Palmer to successfully defend his British Open title.

Like many Americans of his era, he played regularly overseas, particularly in Europe, although he also had success in Japan and Australia. His last victory on the PGA tour was in 1984, but then he began a highly successful second career on the Seniors Tour, where he won 29 titles, including four majors. For a number of years, he also worked as a golf colour analyst for NBC television.

GREATEST ACHIEVEMENTS IN GOLF

- An icon for Mexican Americans, Trevino, who was renowned for his sense of humour, won 92 professional tournaments – 29 on the PGA Tour, five in Europe, one in Japan. He also won 29 senior events, and 28 events of other kinds. He won six Majors, and is one of only four players to win the US Open, the British Open, and the PGA Championship twice, although he never won the Masters.
- In 1966, he was named Rookie of the Year by the PGA.
- He was the first player to shoot all four regulation rounds at the US Open under par in 1968.
- The American was a five time winner of the Harry Vardon Trophy for the lowest scoring average on the PGA Tour.
- In 1971, Trevino was named Sportsman of the Year by Sports Illustrated, voted International Sports Personality of the Year by the BBC, and named Male Athlete of the Year by Associated Press.
- He played in six Ryder Cup teams for the USA, and was the non-playing captain in 1885.
- He also played in six World Cups and was the individual winner of the event in 1969.
- Trevino was inducted into the World Golf Hall of Fame in 1981.
- He has streets in Texas and New Mexico named after him.

GREATEST QUOTES

"My swing is so bad I look like a caveman killing his lunch"

"The older I get, the better I used to be".

"To me, the British Open is the tournament I would come to if had to leave a month before and swim over".

JACK NICKLAUS

MAJORS WON

The Masters	🏆	X6
PGA Championship	🏆	X5
US Open	🏆	X4
The Open	🏆	X3

PGA TOUR VICTORIES	PRO VICTORIES
73	117

Full Name	Jack William Nicklaus
Nickname	The Golden Bear
Nationality	American
Turned Pro	1961

CHILDHOOD

Nicklaus was born in Columbus, Ohio, and is of German descent. His father Charles was a pharmacist, who was also a talented sportsman in his own right, playing American Football at a semi-professional level as well as being a scratch golfer and local tennis champion. His son took the game up at the age of ten, and by the age of 13, was winning local State junior titles. Between the ages of 10 and 17 he won 27 events in the Ohio area.

He attended Ohio State University and initially intended to follow his father into pharmacy, before he switched to study insurance. At first he intended to remain an amateur, but with a family on its way, he changed his mind ·and turned professional in order to support them.

GOLF CAREER

Nicklaus had a meteoric rise to his career. He won the US Open in 1962, and the following year he won the Masters and PGA Championships, as well as a number of other tournaments. For the next four years, he was the best player in the world, and after a brief career downturn, he enjoyed a career resurgence after 1970 that brought him even more success. He had the ability to reinvent his game whenever he suffered a loss of form and was never afraid to go back to the drawing board with his coaches and start again.

He won his sixth Masters at the age of 48, and then turned to the Senior Tour, where again he enjoyed more Major success.

Nicklaus now devotes most of his time to golf course design, and his company is one of the leading designers in the world. He has written a number of books in golf, gave his name to the successful Jack Nicklaus computer game series, and owns Jack Nicklaus gold equipment, which manufacturers a range of golfing equipment designed for golfers with varying abilities. He is also associated with soft drink brands and a range of wines.

GREATEST ACHIEVEMENTS IN GOLF

- Widely considered to be one of the greatest players of all time (if not the greatest), Nicklaus won a record 18 Majors, three more than the next man on the all-time list, Tiger Woods.
- Nicklaus and Woods are the only men to have won three Career Grand Slams.
- He won 117 professional tournaments in his career, and finished with 73 PGA Tour victories, third on the all-time list.
- He holds the record for the most wins at the Masters (six) and the Players' Championship (three).
- No man has played in more majors than Nicklaus (104). He also holds the record for the most runners-up finished in majors (19).
- He was inducted into the World Golf Hall of Fame in 1974 and the Canadian equivalent 21 years later.
- He was awarded the Congressional Gold Medal in 2014.

Among his list of many achievements are:
- In 44 majors from 1970 to 1980, Nicklaus missed just one cut, featuring in 39 successive majors between the 1969 Masters and the 1978 British Open.
- He won five of the first eight senior Major Championships in which he participated.
- At the age of 75, he achieved his first ever hole in one playing in the Masters' par 3 Contest at Augusta.

HARRY VARDON

MAJORS WON

The Masters	🏆	X0
PGA Championship	🏆	X0
US Open	🏆	X1
The Open	🏆	X6

PGA TOUR VICTORIES	PRO VICTORIES
N/A	49

Full Name	Henry William Vardon
Nickname	The Stylist
Nationality	English, Jersey
Turned Pro	1890

CHILDHOOD

Vardon was born in Jersey, in the Channel Islands to an English father and a French mother. Although he did not play much golf as a boy, he showed a natural aptitude for the game when he began to caddie as a teenager. The family's poor financial circumstances held back his golf development and he made the decision to move to England to further his career.

He took a job initially as a greenkeeper, before becoming the club professional the following year at the age of 21. He was a trend setter, with a demanding practice routine, and he wore knickerbockers instead of the usual garb worn by gentleman players at that time – an uncomfortable shirt and buttoned jacket.

GOLF CAREER

Vardon won the first of his six British Open Championships in 1898 (a record that still stands to this day), competing with James Baird and J.H. Taylor, who were part of "The Triumvirate" that dominated golf in the early years of the 20th century, and helped to popularise it. His tour of the United States and Canada in 1900 made him the first golf international celebrity, and he competed in many exhibitions as well as tournaments.

He contracted tuberculosis in 1903, and suffered with health problems after that, turning instead to coaching and writing golf instruction and more broad-themed inspirational books.

When he did return to playing regularly, nerve damage to his right hand impeded his putting ability. Many commentators believe that without that he would have ended his career with many more majors to his name. In later years he became a golf course designer, responsible for several courses in Great Britain.

GREATEST ACHIEVEMENTS IN GOLF

- Vardon is famous for popularising the Vardon grip – or the overlapping grip – which is still the most popular grip used by golfers today (it is a myth that he invented it, with most historians now crediting it to Scotsman Johnny Laidlay, who won the British Amateur Championship in 1889 and 1891).
- He won 49 titles during his career. To go along with this, he also won 21 team events. That was the most by any player up to that point in history. Included in that trophy haul were seven majors – six British Opens and the US Open in 1900. At a time when transatlantic travel was much more difficult than it is now, he made three visits to play in the US Open, finishing second on the two other occasions.
- Between 1898 and 1899, Vardon played in 17 events, won 14 of them, and finished second in the other three.
- One of the original inductees into the Golf Hall of fame, when Vardon died in 1937, the PGA Tour created the Vardon Trophy, awarded annually to the player with the lowest scoring average on tour.
- In addition, the British PGA also created the Harry Vardon Trophy – the award for the winner of the European Tour's Race to Dubai.

GREATEST QUOTES

"Never concede the putt that beats you."

"I'm the best and I'll thank you to remember that."

GREG NORMAN

MAJORS WON

The Masters	🏆	X0
PGA Championship	🏆	X0
US Open	🏆	X0
The Open	🏆	X2

PGA TOUR VICTORIES	PRO VICTORIES
20	91

Full Name	Gregory John Norman
Nickname	The Great White Shark
Nationality	Australian
Turned Pro	1976

CHILDHOOD

Norman was born in Mount Isa, Queensland. His father was Mervin, an electrical engineer, and his mother, Toini. His mother had a single figure handicap herself, so she taught him the game as a teenager and allowed him to caddie for her.

Within 18 months, Norman went from a player with a 27 handicap to a scratch golfer, and he began to attract local media attention. At the age of 20, he became assistant professional at a golf club, and later that same year made the decision to turn pro.

GOLF CAREER

Norman won his first tournament in 1976 in Australia, and joined the European Tour the following year, achieving his first win on that circuit at the Martini International in Scotland. After several years of success competing in Europe, he switched to the PGA Tour, achieving his first victory there in 1984. He became the world's most dominant player, with the only black mark on his CV being his comparative lack of success in majors.

A career slump in the early 1990s saw him remodel his swing with coach Butch Harmon. After this he enjoyed a career revival, winning a second British Open. In 1996, he famously led the Masters by six strokes going into the last round, but blew it and was overtaken by Nick Faldo. He won two tournaments in 1997, but they were his last on the PGA Tour as he began to suffer from a variety of hip, shoulder and back problems. He now believes that he could have avoided some of these issues had he appreciated the importance of golf fitness earlier in his career.

Norman chose not to play the Senior tour, instead concentrating on his business interests. Through his own company, he has been responsible for the creation of more than 100 golf courses across the world. He is also an entrepreneur with a wide portfolio of business interests including wine making, real estate, eye wear, fine dining and water sports.

Norman is currently one of the public figures associated with LIV Golf Investments – a Saudi-backed group which has plans for a series of lucrative events on the Asian Tour, and which is aiming to attract some of the biggest names in the game with inflated prize money and appearance fees.

GREATEST ACHIEVEMENTS IN GOLF

- Norman was the top ranked golfer in the world for much of the 1980s and early 1990s, spending 331 weeks as number one. He won 91 professional tournaments, including 20 on the PGA tour and two majors – the British Open in 1986 and 1993. He also finished runner-up in eight other majors. He was renowned for his aggressive driving style.
- He was leading money winner on the PGA Tour three times, and earned over $1 million on tour five times at the peak of his career.
- He won the Australian Order of Merit six times, and the European equivalent in 1982.
- He won the Vardon Trophy for the lowest scoring average on the PGA tour four times and was inducted into the World Golf Hall of Fame in 2001.
- He was twice named BBC Overseas Sports Personality of the Year.
- He was elevated to legend Status in the Sport Australia Hall of Fame in 2007.
- In 2016, the PGA of Australia inaugurated the Greg Norman Medal, awarded annually to the best male or female Australian golfer in a particular year.

GENE SARAZEN

MAJORS WON

The Masters	🏆	X1
PGA Championship	🏆	X3
US Open	🏆	X2
The Open	🏆	X1

PGA TOUR VICTORIES	PRO VICTORIES
38	48

Full Name	Eugenio Saraceni
Nickname	The Squire/Gene Sarazen
Nationality	American
Turned Pro	1920

CHILDHOOD

Sarazen was born in Harrison, New York. He was the son of poor Sicilian immigrants. He began caddying at a local club when he was ten years old. Here he took up the game himself, and gradually honed his skills, although he was largely self-taught. In his mid-teens he took a series of jobs in the New York area as a golf professional, and then toured playing in tournaments across the East Coast.

GOLF CAREER

In 1922, Sarazen won both the US Open and PGA Championships, and he would go on to win regularly for much of the next two decades. His career overlapped with that of Bobby Jones and Walter Hagen, and the rivalry between the three helped boost the popularity of the sport. In addition to tournaments, Sarazen played in several lengthy and lucrative exhibition tours around the world.

Even when he was no longer winning events, as a past champion he was eligible to continue competing in tournaments, and continued to do so even into his seventies. At the age of 71, he managed a hole in one in 1973 at the Open Championship in Troon. He was a ceremonial starter at the Masters for years and also worked as a TV golf commentator.

GREATEST ACHIEVEMENTS IN GOLF

- Arguably Sarazen's greatest achievement was the invention of the modern sand wedge – the basic design and method he created are used by players all across the world today. Having previously struggled with sand play, his innovation was to weld solder on to the lower back of the club. Meaning that the flange sat lower from the leading edge. He also began to play so that the flange, and not the leading edge, would make contact with the sand first.

- Sarazen won 38 tournaments on the PGA tour, one in Australia, and six other events, plus three as a Senior. He is one of only five players to have completed the Career Grand Slam. He won the PGA Championship three times, the US Open twice, and the Masters and British Open once.

- In 1935 he played the shot "heard round the world" at the Masters when he double eagled the 15th which enabled him to tie with Craig Wood, who he went on to beat in a play-off. Today, the bridge in the 15th at Augusta is named after him.

- Named Associated Press Male Athlete of the Year in 1932, he was the recipient of the PGA's First Lifetime Achievement award in 1996.

- In 1974, he was inducted into the World Golf Hall of Fame.

- He played in six Ryder Cup teams between 1927 and 1937.

- Sarazen still has the longest running endorsement deal in sporting history – 75 years with Wilson Sporting Goods until his death at the age of 97.

GREATEST QUOTES

"I have been able to hope for the best, expect the worst, and take what comes along. If there has been one fundamental reason for my success, this is it."

GARY PLAYER

MAJORS WON

The Masters	🏆	X3
PGA Championship	🏆	X2
US Open	🏆	X1
The Open	🏆	X3

PGA TOUR VICTORIES	PRO VICTORIES
24	160

Full Name	Gary James Player
Nickname	The Black Knight
Nationality	South African
Turned Pro	1953

CHILDHOOD

Player was born in Johannesburg. He is the youngest of three children to Harry and Muriel Player. His mother died when he was eight years old from cancer. His father was often away from home working in South Africa's gold mines, but he managed to get a loan to buy his son his first set of golf clubs. He began playing at a nearby golf course, and by the age of 16 announced his intention to become the number one player in the world. He turned professional the following year.

GOLF CAREER

In 1957 he joined the PGA Tour, registering his first PGA tour win at the Kentucky Derby Open in 1958. He won his first major in 1959, the British Open, and two years later recorded the first of his Masters' victories. The 1980s were his most successful decade, winning more than twenty titles on both the regular and Seniors' tour, including five senior majors. Despite his advancing age, Player continued to enjoy success, winning the Senior Skin Game in 2000 and 2001.

He played in the Augusta Masters for the last time in 2009, appearing for a record 52nd time, but returned as an honorary starter alongside Jack Nicklaus and Arnold Palmer, reuniting the so-called "Big Three".

He faced occasional accusations of cheating during his career, particularly at the British Open in 1974, and nine years later at a skins' game in Arizona, where Tom Watson claimed he had moved a leaf behind a ball. He always strongly denied such allegations.

GREATEST ACHIEVEMENTS IN GOLF

- Player is most famous for becoming the only non-American to win the Grand Slam of Golf. At the time, he was also the youngest ever to do so.
- He won nine majors – Three Masters, Three British Opens, the US Open, and the PGA Championship twice.
- He won 160 professional tournaments in his career over seven decades, and was inducted into the World Golf Hall of Fame in 1974.
- He was the only player in the 20th Century to win the British Open in three different decades.
- He was named South African Sportsman of the Century in 2000, and three years later received the prestigious Laureus Lifetime Achievement Award.
- He was the first golfer to appear on South Africa's postage stamps.
- Player was inducted into the African American Sports Hall of Fame in 2007.
- Four years later, with Jack Nicklaus, he was also inducted into the Asian Pacific Golf Hall of Fame.
- One of the world's foremost golf course designers, he has designed more than 400 courses across the globe.
- He has also authored a number of books on the game, golf course design, motivation and fitness.
- He helped establish the Player Foundation which has the primary objective of promoting education among underprivileged children across the world.
- In 2013 he appeared nude in ESPN The Magazine, the oldest athlete ever to do so, to inspire people to keep look after their bodies, whatever their age.
- In his early years he expresses support for the apartheid policies of the South African government, but later changed his mind claiming that white people of his generation had been brainwashed into backing such policies.

Cary Middlecoff

Majors Won

The Masters		X1
PGA Championship		X0
US Open		X2
The Open		X0

PGA Tour Victories	Pro Victories
39	40

Full Name	Emmett Cary Middlecoff
Nickname	Doc
Nationality	American
Turned Pro	1947

CHILDHOOD

Middlecoff was born in Halls, Tennessee as Emmett Cary Middlecoff. Having graduated from high school, he played collegiate golf at the University of Mississippi. He then enrolled at the University of Tennessee as a dental student whilst competing in local amateur championships. After obtaining his degree as a dentist, he joined the US Army as a dental surgeon during World War II. Middlecoff was selected for the 1947 Walker Cup team, but then immediately withdrew as he had decided to turn professional.

GOLF CAREER

For the next decade or so, no player in the PGA tour was more successful than Cary, although he never won as many majors as commentators felt his game deserved. In later life he proclaimed that winning the 1956 US Open was his greatest achievement, at a time when his powers were just beginning to wane.

As he got older, he began to struggle with nerves, and recurring back problems forced him to retire. He did play occasionally after that competing in the Masters in 1971, which he always regarded as his favourite event. After retiring from competitive play, Middlecoff became one of the earliest golf television commentators, working as a golf analyst for 18 years. He declined to appear in Senior and legends events, preferring privacy and arguing that he had already done enough travelling in his career.

He also appeared in two motion pictures as himself. In 1993 he had a fall at home which resulted in a serious head injury, and he never played a single round of golf after that.

GREATEST ACHIEVEMENTS IN GOLF

- Despite the impediment of having one leg shorter than the other, Middlecoff became one of the top players in the game, renowned for his long iron shots, putting ability and also for the time it took him to make a shot.
- Middlecoff won 40 professional golf tournaments in his career and is tied seventh on the PGA all time list of career victories. He won three majors – the US Open in 1949 and 1956, and the Masters in 1955. He was also twice runner-up in the Masters and once in the PGA Championship.
- Middlecoff won at least one title in 13 out of his 15 years on the PGA tour, with his best years being 1948, 1950, and 1956, recording six wins in each of them.
- No player won more events than him in the 1950s, and he was the leading money earner during that period.
- He won the Vardon Trophy in 1956 for the best shot average on the PGA Tour.
- He appeared in three Ryder Cup teams, and was on the winning side each time.
- He was inducted into the World Golf Hall of Fame, and is also a charter member of the Tennessee Golf Hall of Fame.

GREATEST QUOTES

"I always think before an important shot: What is the worst that can happen on this shot? I can whiff it, shank it, or hit it out of bounds".

"Concentrate on hitting the green. The cup will come to you."

"Anyone who hasn't been nervous, or hasn't choked somewhere down the line, is an idiot".

BYRON NELSON

MAJORS WON

The Masters	🏆	X2
PGA Championship	🏆	X2
US Open	🏆	X1
The Open	🏆	X0

PGA TOUR VICTORIES	PRO VICTORIES
52	64

Full Name	John Byron Nelson Jr.
Nickname	Lord Byron
Nationality	American
Turned Pro	1932

CHILDHOOD

Nelson was born in Waxahachie, Texas, into a very religious family. He was the son of John Byron and Madge Allan Nelson. When he was 11, the family moved to Fort Worth where Byron contracted typhoid fever – he lost half his body weight, and the after-effects meant he was unable to have children. Once recovered, he started caddying at a nearby country club, where one of his fellow caddies was a young Ben Hogan. When Nelson beat Hogan to win a junior tournament, he was offered a club membership, forcing Hogan to move and continue his career elsewhere.

He turned pro in 1932, and worked as a club professional whilst entering as many tournaments as possible in a bid to earn money against the backdrop of the Great Depression.

GOLF CAREER

Nelson's first significant victory was at the New Jersey State Open in 1935, and two years later he claimed the first of his two Masters' titles. His first-round score was the lowest shot at the course until 1976. During the Second World War, a blood disorder rendered him unfit for military service. Instead, he toured the country playing in hundreds of golf exhibitions to raise money for good causes.

In 1946, Nelson retired at the comparatively early age of 34 in order to take up ranching. However, he continued to compete in the occasional tournament, winning the 1951 Bing Crosby Pro-Am and the French Open four years later.

He continued to put on paid exhibition matches and combined that with a career as a golf commentator. He also worked as a coach and mentor for more than two decades.

GREATEST ACHIEVEMENTS IN GOLF

- Nelson won 64 professional tournaments in his career, including five majors: two Masters, two PGA Championships and one US Open.
- In 1945, he finished with 18 victories, including 11 consecutive wins, and established a record for the lowest scoring average that stood for 56 years until Tiger Woods surpassed it. During that year, he played in 30 events, never finishing outside the top ten and coming second seven times.
- He is only one of two golfers to be named Male Athlete of the Year by the Associated Press, and was the first professional golfer to have a tournament named after him.
- In 1939 he won the Vardon Trophy for the best scoring average on the PGA Tour.
- His record of consecutive cuts made (113) is second only to Woods (142).
- He became the first golfer to win 50 PGA tournaments in his career.
- He played on two Ryder Cup teams and was a non-playing captain in 1965.
- Admitted to the World Golf Hall of Fame in 1974, thirty years later he had an exhibit devoted to him which honoured his achievements not only as a champion but also reflected his humanitarian efforts.
- In 2006 he was awarded the Congressional Medal posthumously.

GREATEST QUOTES

"Every great player has learned the two Cs; how to concentrate, and how to maintain composure."

BOBBY JONES

MAJORS WON

The Masters	🏆	X0
PGA Championship	🏆	X0
US Open	🏆	X4
The Open	🏆	X3

PGA TOUR VICTORIES	PRO VICTORIES
9	N/A

Full Name	Robert Tyre Jones Jr.
Nickname	Calamity Jane
Nationality	American
Turned Pro	Never

CHILDHOOD

Born in Atlanta, Georgia, Jones suffered from a range of health issues as a boy, and his father "Colonel" Robert Purmedos Jones, a lawyer, encouraged him to take up golf to help make him stronger. He proved to be a natural at the game and developed into a child prodigy, winning his first junior competition at the age of six. Eight years later he claimed his inaugural senior amateur title, and began to play in exhibition events, although he had to learn how to control a temper that sometimes got out of control on the course.

In 1919 and 1920, he successfully represented the United States in two amateur events against Canada, and then qualified for the US Open for the first time. He won the Southern Amateur title three times – in 1917, 1920, and 1922.

GOLF CAREER

Jones' career is divided into two parts – the "Seven Lean Years" and the "Seven Fat Years". The first period covered the ages 14 to 21 and the second the succeeding seven years. During the first era, he rarely won anything significant, famously becoming so frustrated with play at the 1921 British Open that he picked up the ball and walked off the course. There were also numerous incidents of him throwing his clubs in anger.

However, he finally made the breakthrough by winning the US Open in 1923 and, in the next seven years, he played in 21 national championships and won 13 of them. In 1930 he won the Grand Slam - the US Open, US Amateur Championship,

British Open and British Amateur all in the same year - the first man to do so.

However, at the age of 28 he decided to retire from competitive golf, tired of the mental strain which he compared to being like a caged animal. Having designed the course, he did play in the First Masters and returned to Augusta on a number of occasions, but he was regarded as largely a ceremonial player by then. Gradually he began to suffer from back pain, and this developed into a spinal condition known as syringomyelia. He played his last round of golf in 1948, and spent much of his later years confined to a wheelchair.

GREATEST ACHIEVEMENTS IN GOLF

- Jones won seven majors – the US Open four times (a record equaled by three other men – Willie Anderson, Ben Hogan and Jack Nicklaus), and the British Open three times.
- In addition, he was US Amateur Championship five times – a record, and won the British Amateur Championship as well.
- He was renowned for becoming the first man to win the Grand Slam – victory in all four major golf tournaments of his era – the US and British Opens and the two Amateur Championships.
- He also won 21 other tournaments in his career stretching over 22 years.
- He also finished runner-up at the US Open on four occasions.
- Jones has been consistently rated among the greatest golfers of all times, and is regarded as the most successful amateur player ever.
- After retiring from competitive golf at a comparatively young age, he founded and helped design the Augusta National golf course.

KATHY WHITWORTH

MAJORS WON

Western Open	🏆	X1
Titleholders Championship	🏆	X2
Women's PGA Championship	🏆	X3
US Women's Open	🏆	X0

LPGA TOUR VICTORIES	PRO VICTORIES
88	98

Full Name	Kathrynne Ann Whitworth
Nickname	Miss W
Nationality	American
Turned Pro	1958

CHILDHOOD

Whitworth was born in Monahans, Texas, where her father owned a hardware store, but spent most of her childhood in New Mexico. She came to golf comparatively late at the age of 15, but by the time she graduated from high school she was already New Mexico State Amateur champion, winning it again in 1955. She briefly attended college in Texas, before she turned pro in 1958.

GOLF CAREER

It took her four years to win her first tournament (the 1962 Kelly Girls Open), but after she made the breakthrough, her career really took off. She won at least one tournament every year between 1962 to 1978, with a purple patch in the middle of this stretch. In 1965 she recorded eight wins, nine in 1966, eight in 1967 and ten in 1968.

1984 was her last big year on tour, when she won three tournaments, although she did win once more at the 1985 United Virginia Bank Classic which would be her last. Her record of 88 tour wins, was more than any other player had achieved on any of golf's major world tours, with the exception of the 94 wins that Jumbo Ozaki notched up on the Japanese Tour.

During her career, Whitworth was renowned as both an excellent driver and fine putter, and although some have claimed her record in majors was modest compared to her talent, for much of the time she was playing there were only two majors on the LPGA Tour.

She retired from competitive golf in 2005 after competing in the BJ's Charity Classic on the Seniors Tour, and went on to become a highly regarded teacher of the game.

GREATEST ACHIEVEMENTS IN GOLF

- Whitworth won 88 LPGA Tour titles, six more than the next name on the all-time list, Mickey Wright. Her tournament haul included six major championships – the Women's PGA Championship three times, the Titleholders twice, and the Western Open.
- She was eight times the tour money leader, and was named LPGA Player of the Year on seven occasions. In addition, she won the LGPA Vare Trophy for the best scoring average on tour seven times.
- In 1981, Whitworth became the first female golfer to exceed $1 million career earnings when she finished third at the US Women's Open.
- Her record of at least one tournament victory every year for 17 years is the longest winning streak in LPGA history.
- She was named Associated Press Athlete of the Year in 1965, and again two years later, and captained the US Solheim Cup Team in 1990 and again in 1992.
- A member of the World Golf Hall of Fame, she served three terms as LPGA president. There she is remembered for helping to shape policy and campaigned for the growth of the LGPA tour.

GREATEST QUOTES

"There are no absolutes in golf. Golf is such an individual game and no two people swing alike."

"Golf is a game of misses, and the winners are those who have the best misses".

ARNOLD PALMER

MAJORS WON

The Masters		X4
PGA Championship		X0
US Open		X1
The Open		X2

PGA TOUR VICTORIES	PRO VICTORIES
62	95

Full Name	Arnold Daniel Palmer
Nickname	The King
Nationality	American
Turned Pro	1954

CHILDHOOD

Palmer was born in Latrobe, Pennsylvania in a working-class steel mill town. His father was Milton Jerome 'Deacon" and his mother was Doris Palmer. He learned golf from his father who was head professional and greenskeeper at a local country club. He attended Wake Forest College on a golf scholarship, but left after the death of a close friend and enlisted in the US Coast Guard where he served for three years. Whilst serving with them, he built a nine-hole course, and when his enlistment ended, he returned to college and competitive golf. He won the US Amateur title in 1954 and turned pro later that same year.

GOLF CAREER

Palmer's first professional win came during his rookie year when he won the Canadian Open in 1955. His first major championship win came in 1958 at the Masters, cementing his position as one of the leading stars of the sport. Coupled with this, his modest background, handsome appearance, willingness to wear his heart on the sleeve and his involvement in a number of close tournament finishes soon made him a household name.

Palmer is also credited with making the British Open more popular with American players. Due to the distances involved and the relatively small purse on offer, few had bothered to travel to the UK before he set the example. It ensured his immense popularity also among British and European fans. His most successful years on tour were between 1960 and 1963, where he won 29 PGA Tour events in four seasons. In 1967, he became the first man to amass $1 million in career earnings, and although other players would later pass him in terms of world rankings, he won at least one tour event each year between 1955 and 1971.

When he became eligible for the Senior PGA Tour in its inaugural season in 1980, he was one of the first players that helped establish the popularity of that as well. In 2004 he competed in the Masters for the last time, his 50th consecutive appearance in the tournament. He retired from golf in 2006, but was honorary starter at the Masters from 2007 until his death in 2016.

GREATEST ACHIEVEMENTS IN GOLF

- Palmer was the first superstar of the sport in the television age, with his charisma and personality responsible more than any other player for bringing it to a mass audience. In a career spanning six decades, he won 95 tournaments, including 62 on the PGA Tour.
- He won seven majors – the Masters four times, the US Open once and the British Open twice.
- Palmer finished with career earnings of $6.9 million.
- He was PGA Player of the year in 1960 and 1962, and the leading money winner on the PGA Tour four times.
- Palmer won the Vardon Trophy (awarded to the PGA Tour's leader in scoring average on four separate occasions, and was a member of the victorious Ryder Cup team six times, captaining the side in 1963 and 1975. He was also the President's Cup Captain in 1966 and featured and skippered the UBS Team between 2001 and 2004.
- He achieved 20 holes in one, and his biggest winning margin was by 12 strokes at the Phoenix Open in 1962.

Annika Sörenstam

Majors Won

ANA Inspiration	🏆	X3
Women's PGA Championship	🏆	X3
US Women's Open	🏆	X3
Women's British Open	🏆	X1

LPGA Tour Victories	Pro Victories
72	90

Full Name	Annika Charlotta Sörenstam
Nickname	Ms. 59
Nationality	Swedish
Turned Pro	1992

CHILDHOOD

Sörenstam was born in Bro near Stockholm. Her father Tom was an executive with IBM, and her mother, Gunilla, worked in a bank. She has a younger sister, Charlotte, who also became a professional golfer, and was successful in her own right, winning on the LPGA tour. The two sisters would become the first two siblings to each earn over $1 million on the LGPA tour.

She was a talented athlete as a child, excelling in many sports including tennis, football and skiing. She also began playing golf at a local club. As a youngster, she was so shy she would deliberately three putt in tournaments to avoid giving victory speeches, before her coaches noticed this and she learned how to cope with the public pressure.

GOLF CAREER

The Swede attended the University of Arizona, where in 1991, she won a National Collegiate Association title, and was twice an all-American. The following year she won the World Amateur Championship, finished second at the US Women's Amateur Championship and posted the second lowest score by an amateur at that year's US Women's Open. In 1993, she was named Rookie of the Year on the European Tour, and the following year, received the same accolade on the US tour.

Her first LGPA victory came in 1995 at the US Women's Open, resulting in her being named Player of the Year. Over the next decade, she would earn that honour seven more times. In 1998 she became the first player on the LGPA tour to finish the season with a scoring average below 70.

Three years later she won eight LGPA events, and became the first woman to score 59 in a round of a professional tournament (hence her nickname).

Her eleven wins in the 2002 season was the best on the LGPA tour for nearly 40 years, and the following year she completed the career Grand Slam of major victories. That same year she became the first woman to play in a men's Professional Golf Association tournament. She retired from professional golf in 2008.

GREATEST ACHIEVEMENTS IN GOLF

- Sörenstam is regarded as one of the best female golfers in history.
- When she retired from the game, she won 90 international tournaments (the most by any female), including 72 on the official LPGA tour. That haul included 10 majors. The Swede tops the all-time LPGA career money list, with earnings in excess of $22 million – $2 million ahead of her nearest rival, the Australian Karrie Webb, who played in 187 more events than her.
- The winner of a record eight Player of the Year awards, she also won six Vare Trophies, awarded to the woman with the lowest scoring average in a season.
- Internationally, playing for Europe in the Solheim Cup, she was the event's all-time leading point scorer for many years, and was captain of the team in 2017.
- A member of the Golf Hall of Fame, she received the Presidential Medal of Freedom in January 2021 by President Donald Trump.

GREATEST QUOTES

"I push myself to be the best I can be. I don't worry about what other people are doing, and I don't think about things I can't control".

BEN HOGAN

MAJORS WON

The Masters	🏆	X2
PGA Championship	🏆	X2
US Open	🏆	X4
The Open	🏆	X1

PGA TOUR VICTORIES	PRO VICTORIES
64	71

Full Name	William Ben Hogan
Nickname	The Wee Ice Man
Nationality	American
Turned Pro	1930

CHILDHOOD

Ben Hogan was born in Stephenville, Texas. His father, Chester, was a blacksmith but committed suicide in front of him when he was nine years old. The family faced financial problems after that and Hogan and his two siblings took odd jobs to help his mother Clara make ends meet. A tip from a friend led him into caddying when he was 11 years old, where one of his fellow caddies was Byron Nelson, a rival later on tour.

Nelson was granted the only junior membership offered by their local club. Hogan switched his allegiance to another club. He dropped out of high school in his final senior year and turned pro just before his 18th birthday, in January 1930.

GOLF CAREER

Hogan initially struggled as a golf pro during the era of the Great Depression, and did not win his first tournament until 1940, struggling to control a troublesome hook. However, from there until 1959, he won 63 professional tournaments, despite the interruption to his career of the Second World War. He also survived a near fatal car accident with his wife, that at the age of 36 left him with a double fracture of the pelvis, a fractured collar bone and ankle, a chipped rib and life-threatening blood clots.

Some thought he might not play golf again but he recovered, and in 1953 won five of the six tournaments he entered. This included the Triple Crown – the Masters, the US Open and the British Open – the only man to win three majors in one year until Tiger Woods emulated it in 2000.

Widely acknowledged as one of the greatest ball strikers of all time, he claimed in later life to have discovered a secret that made his swing almost automatic. However, especially after his car accident, which affected his vision in his left eye, he had problems with his putting, especially on slow greens, and also struggled with the "yips".

GREATEST ACHIEVEMENTS IN GOLF

- Hogan achieved 64 PGA Tour wins, plus a further seven in other tournaments. He won nine majors – two PGA Championships, four US Opens, the Masters twice and the British Open once.
- He played on two Ryder Cup teams, one as captain, and was non-playing captain on two further occasions.
- He won the Vardon Trophy for the lowest scoring average on tour three times.
- In 1974 he was inducted into the World Golf Hall of Fame, and two years later, was given the Bobby Jones Award for the USGA for distinguished sportsmanship. A room dedicated to him and his achievements can be found at the United States Golf Association Museum in New Jersey.
- There is also a Ben Hogan Museum in his childhood hometown which pays tribute to the legendary golfer.
- Every year, the Golf Writers Association of America gives the Ben Hogan award to a player who has remained active despite a physical handicap or serious illness.
- In 1953 he founded his own golf club company, and it still continues to this day, although not in its original form.

GREATEST QUOTES

"The most important shot in golf is the next one".

"A shot that goes in the cup is pure luck, but a shot to within two feet of the flag is skill."

PHIL MICKELSON

MAJORS WON

The Masters		X3
PGA Championship		X2
US Open		X0
The Open		X1

PGA TOUR VICTORIES	PRO VICTORIES
45	57

Full Name	Philip Alfred Mickelson
Nickname	Lefty
Nationality	American
Turned Pro	1992

CHILDHOOD

Mickelson was born in San Diego, California to Mary Santos, and Philip Mickelson, an airline pilot and former navy aviator. His maternal grandfather worked as a caddie at a local links course and took Phil to play golf there when he was still a boy. Naturally right-handed, Mickelson began to play left-handed by watching his father's swing and mirroring it. Thanks to his father's works schedule, the pair were able to play several times a week, and helped him hone his short game.

He attended Arizona State University on a golf scholarship, and became a highly successful amateur golfer, winning numerous championships. A four time all-American, he became only the sixth amateur to win a tour event at the Western Open in 1985. He graduated from college in 1992 and turned professional soon afterwards.

GOLF CAREER

Although he won a number of tournaments in his early years, his inability to win a major earned him the reputation as "the best player to never win a major." However, he ended that sequence with victory at the Masters in 2004, sinking an 18-foot birdie putt on the final green. He won the PGA Championship the following year, and the Masters for the second time the year later.

Although he continued to be one of the world's top golfers, the US Open title has continually eluded him, finishing runner-up six times. Between 2013 and 2018 he went winless on the PGA tour, a streak that was ended at the WGC championship in Mexico.

He became the oldest major champion in 2021 wining the PGA championship and finished the year by winning the season ending Charles Schwab Cup Championship in Phoenix.

Most recently, he has vented his frustration with the PGA tour accusing them of "obnoxious" greed and has threatened to join the new league being formed under the auspices of Greg Norman unless the organisation ceded control of media rights back to the players.

GREATEST ACHIEVEMENTS IN GOLF

- Mickelson has 45 PGA tour victories, placing him eighth on the all-time list. He has won six majors, including three Masters, and in 2021, became the oldest ever winner of a major when he beat the field by two strokes to win the PGA Championship (he was 50 years, 11 months and 7 days old).
- He has finished runner-up at the US Open a record six times.
- Although he is second on the all-time list of money earnings on the PGA Tour, that is dwarfed by what he makes off it – he has earned at least US $750 million from endorsements, appearance fees and golf course design fees.
- He spent 26 consecutive years in the top 50 of the Official World Golf ranking, a streak that was finally ended in November 2019.
- He has featured in 12 Ryder Cup and 12 President Cup teams.
- Between 2004 and 2013 he won at least one tournament each year.

GREATEST QUOTES

"The object of golf is not just to win. It is to play like a gentleman and win".

SAM SNEAD

MAJORS WON

The Masters		X3
PGA Championship		X3
US Open		X0
The Open		X1

PGA TOUR VICTORIES	PRO VICTORIES
82	142

Full Name	Samuel Jackson Snead
Nickname	Slammin' Sammy
Nationality	American
Turned Pro	1934

CHILDHOOD

Snead was born in Ashwood, Virginia. He began caddying at the age of seven at a local course, and during the Great Depression taught himself how to play golf using a set of clubs fashioned from bits of tree. By the age of 17, he was working as an assistant professional at the Homestead club.

He turned professional in 1934, joining the PGA tour two years later, achieving almost immediate success by winning a local tournament.

GOLF CAREER

In 1936 he won his first tournament, the West Virginia Closed pro, beginning a winning sequence on the PGA Tour that would last until 1965. Snead became one of the most recognisable players on tour, not only because of his swing, but also because he frequently wore a straw hat and came out with a number of folksy sayings, such as 'keep close count of your nickels and dimes' and 'never concede a putt'. He would have won more during the Second World War years, but many events, including 14 Major Championships, were cancelled during that time. Snead himself served in the US navy between 1942 and 1944.

He resumed his career and his winning run after the end of the fighting, winning nine PGA events in 1949, eleven the following year, and ten the year after that. He continued to play deep into old age, and in 1997 at the age of 85, he shot a round of 78 at a course in West Virginia.

GREATEST ACHIEVEMENTS IN GOLF

- Snead was one of the top players in the world for almost four decades, and is credited with having a record 82 PGA Tour wins (in addition to 12 other sanctioned events). He won seven majors, the only one to elude him being the US Open, where he was runner-up four times.
- He was the PGA leading money winner three times, and won the Vardon Trophy for the lowest scoring average on the PGA Tour on four occasions.
- He was named PGA Player of the Year in 1949.
- Snead was renowned for his long rhythmic swing (Gary Player described it as the best ever) but had a reputation for being a mediocre putter, something he blamed on using his wrists instead of his arms.
- He was the first player to win an event 17 times – the West Virginia Open between 1936 and 1973.
- Snead was the first player to be credited with winning a PGA Tour event in four different decades, and the oldest player to win a PGA tournament, winning the 1965 Greater Greensboro Open when he was almost 53.
- He was the oldest player to make the cut on the PGA Tour (aged 67), and the only player across five different decades, to post a top ten finish in at least one major.
- He played on seven Ryder Cup teams and was selected for an eighth in 1939, but that was never held because of the outbreak of war in Europe.
- Snead was inducted into the World Golf Hall of Fame in 1953.
- He was given a PGA Lifetime Award in 1998, and between 1984 and 2002 he was the honorary starter at the Masters.
- In 1962, at the age of 49, he won the so-called "Battle of the Swans" in which he took part in a tournament against 14 players from the LPGA tour. Mickey Wright finished runner-up.
- He wrote several golf instructional books, as well as columns in golf magazines, and was the host of a popular Celebrity Golf television programme for a number of years.

WALTER HAGEN

MAJORS WON

The Masters	🏆	X0
PGA Championship	🏆	X5
US Open	🏆	X2
The Open	🏆	X4

PGA TOUR VICTORIES	PRO VICTORIES
45	58

Full Name	Walter Charles Hagen
Nickname	The Haig
Nationality	American
Turned Pro	1912

CHILDHOOD

Hagen was born in Rochester, New York, into a working-class family of German descent. His father worked as a blacksmith and millwright. Hagen began caddying at a nearby country club, which is where he learned the game, earning money to help support his family before he was a teenager. By the time he was in his mid-teens, thanks to coaching from the head professional at the club, he was an expert player and began to give lessons to other members. He made his top-class professional debut in 1912 at the 1912 Canadian Open.

GOLF CAREER

In 1913 he entered the US Open and finished fourth, but was so upset how he was treated by the other professionals that he vowed to return the following year and win it, which he did. He would continue to play and win tournaments for the next 22 years, although his peak years were in the early 1920s, particularly 1924 when he won both the British Open and the PGA Championship. His last tournament win was the Inverness Invitational Four-Ball in 1936, when he was nearly 44 years old.

During his career, his skills were much in demand and he found that he could make more money playing in exhibition matches than he could in many tournaments at the time. He also earned significant sums from endorsing golf equipment, and formed a lucrative partnership with Wilson Sports, helping to design clubs which bore his name. When he died of throat cancer in 1969, Arnold Palmer was one of the pall-bearers at his funeral.

GREATEST ACHIEVEMENTS IN GOLF

- Hagen is regarded as one of the key figures in the development of professional golf, in an era when golf professionals were not allowed to enter clubhouses. He was determined that professionals should have the same status as amateurs and, at one event, refused to go into the clubhouse to collect his prize because he had been denied access to it during the tournament itself.

- Known as the "father of professional golf", he conferred prestige on the sport and helped attract big prize money and lucrative endorsements into the game.

- He was the first golfer to earn $1 million in his career.

- Hagen recorded 58 career wins, 45 on the PGA tour and 13 in other events. He won 11 majors – the US Open twice, the British Open four times, and the PGA Championship on five occasions – putting him third on the all-time list. Only Jack Nicklaus and Tiger Woods have won more. (Some commentators argue that he should be credited with five more majors, winning the Western Open five times during an era when this was considered one of the premier events on the golf schedule).

- He also had three more second place finishes in majors and made the top ten on 44 occasions.

- Hagen played on the first five Ryder Cup teams for the USA, all of them as captain, returning in 1937 in a non-playing role.

- He was one of the original inductees into the Golf Hall of Fame.

GREATEST QUOTES

"You're only here for a short visit. Don't hurry, don't worry. And be sure to smell the flowers along the way".

Make the hard ones look easy, and the easy ones look hard".

"No one remembers who came in second".

BILLY CASPER

MAJORS WON

The Masters	🏆	X1
PGA Championship	🏆	X0
US Open	🏆	X2
The Open	🏆	X0

PGA TOUR VICTORIES	PRO VICTORIES
51	71

Full Name	William Earl Casper Jr.
Nickname	Buffalo Bill
Nationality	American
Turned Pro	1954

CHILDHOOD

Casper was born in San Diego, California. He was the only child of William Earl and Isabel Casper. Encouraged by his father, he began playing golf at the age of five, and during his youth he caddied at a local country club to earn money. He spent one semester at the University of Notre Dame on a golf scholarship before returning to California in 1952 to marry his wife, Shirley. After several years on the amateur circuit, he turned pro in 1954.

GOLF CAREER

Two years after turning professional, he won his first tournament on the PGA tour, beginning a run that would continue for the best part of two decades. Although never one of the 'Big Three" of the time (Nicklaus, Player and Palmer), he still averaged 2.55 wins per year on tour, and at his peak was winning more frequently than any of his rivals.

Only his comparative lack of success in majors meant he was not regarded more highly – either by contemporaries, or by history. Despite this, he retired with a tour record better than luminaries of the game like Walter Hagan, Gene Sarazen and Tom Watson.

Following the end of his playing career, Casper became a highly successful golf course designer. He was also active in charity work and had a cameo role in the Hollywood movie "Now You See Him, Now You Don't."

GREATEST ACHIEVEMENTS IN GOLF

- Casper ranks seventh in terms of all-time PGA Tour wins, winning 51 times between 1956 and 1975, including three majors (two US Open titles and one Masters). He also won two more majors on the Senior tour.

- He was PGA Player of the Year twice and leading money winner on the PGA tour in 1966 and again two years later. Casper also won the Vardon Trophy for the best average score on tour on five occasions.

- He won at least one PGA tour event every year for 16 straight seasons between 1956 to 1971, and was the first PGA Tour player to earn more than $200,000 in a single season.

- He was a member of eight Ryder Cup teams as a player, and was a nonplaying captain in 1979. No American player has ever scored more points in the Ryder Cup for his team.

- He was inducted into the Golf Hall of fame in 1978. He was widely considered to be the best putter of his generation, although some feel he never received the recognition he deserved, and he was overshadowed by the achievements of his contemporaries - Jack Nicklaus, Gary Player and Arnold Palmer.

- The management company he founded, Billy Casper Golf, is the second largest manager of golf courses in the United States. It annually hosts the "World's Largest Golf Outing" – a US national golf fundraiser which benefits military charities.

GREATEST QUOTES

"Golfers are the greatest worriers in the world of sport."

"Think ahead: Golf is a next shot game".

"Golf puts a man's character on the anvil, and his richest qualities – patience, poise, restraint – to the flame".

PATTY BERG

MAJORS WON

Western Open	🏆	X7
Titleholders Championship	🏆	X7
Women's PGA Championship	🏆	X0
US Women's Open	🏆	X1

LPGA TOUR VICTORIES	PRO VICTORIES
60	63

Full Name	Patricia Jane Berg
Nickname	Dynamite
Nationality	American
Turned Pro	1940

CHILDHOOD

Berg was born in Minneapolis, Minnesota, and at an early age, developed a love for American football - playing quarterback on a local team. She began playing golf at the age of 13 at the suggestion of her parents, and within three years was competing in amateur events, claiming the state title in in 1935.

She attended the University of Minnesota and came to national attention when she was runner-up in the 1935 US Women's Western Amateur Championship. After winning 29 amateur titles, including three consecutive Titleholders Championship, she turned professional in 1940.

GOLF CAREER

Berg's career suffered an early setback when she was injured in an automobile accident in 1941, which shattered her knee. She recovered and volunteered as a reserve with the US Marine Corps whilst returning to the game in 1943, although that was almost by accident. She slipped and fell in a locker room and that helped break adhesions which had developed in her leg.

She enjoyed almost immediate success, winning the Women's Western Open, and then won the inaugural US Women's Open in 1948. In 1950, she was one of the 13 founding members of the LPGA. Her last title came in 1962 at the Muskogee Civilian Open.

During her lifetime she taught at over 16,000 golf clinics, and later claimed that she was responsible for more than half a million people taking up the sport.

GREATEST ACHIEVEMENTS IN GOLF

- Berg had 63 career victories, 22 of which came before the LPGA was founded in 1944. She won a record 15 major championships in her career, the first of which was in 1937, when she was still an amateur.
- That record includes a record seven Titleholders' Championships, seven Women's Western Opens and the US Women's Open.
- She was three times the leading money winner on the LGPA tour, and a three-time winner of the Golf Digest Performance Average Award.
- Berg represented the United States in the Curtis Cup in 1936, and again in 1938.
- In 1959 she became the first woman to record a hole in one in a USGA competition at the US Women's Open. 32 years later, at the age of 73, she got another ace.
- Berg was the recipient of the prestigious Bobby Jones Award in 1963, in recognition of her distinguished sportsmanship in golf.
- Berg was one of the original inductees into the LPGA Tour Hall of Fame, and served as the organisations first president between 1950 and 1952, having helped found it in the first place.
- In 2002 she was the honorary chairperson of the Solheim Cup, which was held in New Jersey at her home course, and she raised the American flag during the opening ceremony.
- The Patty Berg, named after her, is given annually by the LPGA to an individual who exhibits the characteristics of diplomacy, sportsmanship, goodwill and makes a significant contribution to the game of golf.

SEVE BALLESTEROS

MAJORS WON

The Masters	🏆	X2
PGA Championship	🏆	X0
US Open	🏆	X0
The Open	🏆	X3

PGA TOUR VICTORIES	PRO VICTORIES
9	90

Full Name	Severiano Ballesteros Sota
Nickname	The Car Park Champion
Nationality	Spanish
Turned Pro	1974

CHILDHOOD

Ballesteros was born in the village of Pedreña, Cantabria, Spain. His parents both worked on a farm as labourers. The youngest of five sons, all but one of them would go on to become professional golfers. Seve learned the game using a club given to him by one of his older brothers, practicing whilst he was meant to be in school.

Golf ran in the family – his maternal uncle was Spanish professional champion four times, and finished sixth in the Masters in 1964, and his nephew Raúl is also a professional golfer. Seve Ballesteros turned professional when he was 16-years old.

GOLF CAREER

He first came to prominence when he finished second at the British Open in 1976, and went on to win the European Tour Order of Merit that year. He won his first major, the 1979 British Open, despite famously hitting his tee shot on the 18th hole in his final round into the car park.

Four more majors – two Masters and two British Opens – were to follow between 1980 and 1988. His Masters win in 1980 was the first by a European player, and he was the youngest winner at that time (although Tiger Woods subsequently eclipsed his record). He had two seasons on the PGA Tour, but preferred playing in Europe.

When European players were allowed to enter the Ryder Cup – previously it had been the USA versus Britain and Ireland – he soon became a mainstay in the team. His partnership with fellow Spaniard Jose Maria Olazabal was the most successful in the history of the competition.

By the late 1990s Ballesteros began to develop back problems, which limited the amount of golf he could play. A recurrence of such issues forced him to officially retire from the sport in 2007. In later years, he became involved in golf course design, and helped in the construction of many courses across Europe. He died in 2011, three years after he was diagnosed with a brain tumour.

GREATEST ACHIEVEMENTS IN GOLF

- Few players have done more to popularise golf, especially in Europe, than Ballesteros. This was due to his charisma, good looks, ingenious shot making and courageous play. He never took the safe option when there was a bolder choice on offer, meaning that he constantly flirted with disaster. However, when it came off, it was spectacular.
- No man did more to change the history of the Ryder Cup and make it into one of the most famous sporting events in the world.
- He was the number one golfer in the world in 1983 and 1984, and again in 1988. He won 50 European Tour titles which is a record, and between 1976 and 1992 he won at least one event each year, a winning streak of 17 years!
- Ballesteros was inducted into the World Golf Hall of Fame in 1999, and was named BBC Sports Personality of the Year in 2000.
- He received numerous civilian awards in Spain, the Olympic Order of Merit, and was given an honorary doctorate by St. Andrews' University.
- In 2000 he was named Spanish Athlete of the Century.
- The airport in his homeland of Cantabria has been renamed after him, whilst the European Tour Players' Player of the Year award also bears his name.